BHAGAVAD GITA

CHANTING GUIDELINES
wrt Panini's Ashtadhyayi

SADHVI HEMSWAROOPA
Ashwini Kumar Aggarwal

जय गुरुदेव

ISBN13: 978-93-95766-26-5 Paperback Edition
ISBN13: 978-93-95766-27-2 Hardbound Edition
ISBN13: 978-93-95766-25-8 Digital Edition

Title: Bhagavad Gita Chanting guidelines wrt Panini's Ashtadhyayi
Author: **Ashwini Kumar Aggarwal, Sadhvi Hemswaroopa**

Printed and Published by
Devotees of Sri Sri Ravi Shankar Ashram
34 Sunny Enclave, Devigarh Road,
Patiala 147001, Punjab, India

https://advaita56.weebly.com/
The Art of Living Centre

https://www.artofliving.org/

25th Dec 2022 Sunday, Merry Christmas, Shukla Paksha, Shishir Ritu, Pausha Masa, Tritiya upari Dvitiya tithi, Uttara Ashadha Nakshatra, Dakshinayana, Tri Pushkara Yoga, Sarvartha Siddhi Yoga.
On this day in 352AD Xmas is officially declared, 800AD Charlemagne is crowned Roman emperor, 1066 William-Norse Viking descent crowned emperor of England, 1656 Christiaan Huygens makes pendulum clock, 1741 Anders Celsius introduces centigrade temperature scale, 1861 Madan Mohan Malaviya's birth, 1962 Premiere of Harper Lee's to kill a mocking bird, 2021 NASA launches James Webb telescope. Vikram Samvat 2079 Nala, Saka Era 1944 Shubhakrit

1st Edition December 2022

जय गुरुदेव

Dedication

H H Sri Sri Ravi Shankar

whose discourse on the Bhagavad Gita is unparalleled

An offering at His Lotus feet

Acknowledgements

Adapted from our popular title 'Bhagavad Gita as Recited vs as Written', to give the gist of the mechanics involved.

Blessing

If you chase desire after desire, it makes you weak, restless and leaves you without peace. Like an ocean, be fulfilled within yourself, and just see how whatever you need, will come to you spontaneously. Like the rivers flow into the ocean, so does your life. This is the Brahman state.

H H Sri Sri Ravi Shankar
Discourse on Gita 7th Chapter in Hindi, 4 to 6 Sep 2015
Yamuna Sports Complex, Delhi

Table of Contents

Prayer

ॐ नमो भगवते वासुदेवाय

ॐ नमो भगवते वासुदेवाय

ॐ नमो भगवते वासुदेवाय

ॐ नमो भगवते वासुदेवाय

oṃ namo bhagavate vāsudevāya
o.m namo bhagavate vaasudevaaya
o.m namo bhagavate vaasudevaaya
o.m namo bhagavate vaasudevaaya

Introduction

Sanskrit words in a sentence coalesce due to conjuncts, sandhis or compounding. Hence written Sanskrit is **slightly different** than spoken Sanskrit. As such a teacher is required for one to learn how to chant the Bhagavad Gita.

The various editions of the Gita generally do not give the Gita as it is to be chanted. These in fact give the Gita as it is to be written in correct grammar! That is useful for contemplation, meditation and going within, and attaining Divine Union.

However for reading or study we need to read aloud and chant loudly. This is when this book becomes very useful.

Remember, the key is to allow the expression to flow. After a few times, sing freely, allowing your natural rhythm to take over.

As you chant confidently, when Devotion seeps into your Being, know you are already there!

The traditional way to Recite the Bhagavad Gita is to
- begin with Gita dhyanam shlokas
- then chant the Gita verses
- end with Gita mahatmayam

This is known as Parayanam.

Gurudev Sri gave us a user-friendly Prayer invocation and ending Prayer that is mentioned in this book.

Most of the Gita verses are written in Anushtup Chhanda with 32 syllables in each verse. Chanting the verses means p a u s i n g after every 8 syllables, thus there will be 4 padas for each verse, i.e. 2 padas for each sentence.

- ➤ This means that **Sandhi** if any present at a p a u s e, will **revert back** or **become different** while c h a n t i n g.

- ➤ Similarly, if any Conjunct was present in a continuous sentence, it is now separated at the point of p a u s e. However this will be only visually different, without change in sounding.

- ➤ Whereas a Samasa is not separated, E.g.
  सुहृन्मित्रार्युदासीन-मध्यस्थद्वेष्यबन्धुषु । 6.9

  जन्ममृत्युजराव्याधि-दुःखदोषानुदर्शनम् ॥ 13.8
  chant this entire sentence without significant pause

- ➤ In some verses, a hyphen has been inserted. Just to split the long words or some conjuncts to enable the reader to see clearly and chant correctly. *It does not indicate samasa or any grammar.* E.g. verse 13.11 अध्यात्म-ज्ञान-नित्यत्वम् , तत्त्व-ज्ञानार्थ-दर्शनम् । verse 13.18 मद्-भावायोप-पद्यते ॥

- ➤ Pausing at the right place during chanting is what lends beauty to the chant, and enlivens the surrounding aura immensely.

This edition is a tremendous aid to self-study learners who wish to see each letter clearly and know the exact pauses. It also serves as an invaluable school and college textbook.

Chanting Guidelines

- See and Chant each LETTER clearly and loudly
- Pay special attention to Conjuncts and Visarga
- Notice the Halant, the Long Matra and the Pause

- Some schools teach sweetness of Anushtup Chhand tune, whereas other schools teach correctness of chanting as per Sanskrit Grammar rules
- Take the middle path of sweetness+correctness

- Learn the right method initially
- Do not hesitate to stop and redo
- Practice is a must

Respect your own mother tongue and your own fluent style of speech, and incorporate whatever you can happily.

Following characters need special attention while chanting

Avagraha ऽ is not to be chanted, i.e. it is a silent letter.
It signifies that an अ has been dropped due to sandhi.

e.g. Recite प्रथमोऽध्यायः as प्रथमोध्यायः ,

verse 2.14 आगमापयिनोऽनित्याः as आगमापयिनोनित्याः , etc.

Visarga ◌ः is pronounced variously, a brief mention

A visarga is pronounced aspirated ह् followed by the

sound of the preceding vowel. Thus नमः is to be

chanted as नमह

This rule is valid only when a visarga is at the end, i.e. a virama is present. This rule also applies when a visarga is followed by a pause, at a quarter verse.

However, a visarga in close proximity with another letter gets replaced by another letter or even gets dropped. This is reflected in this book by substituting the changed letter. (popular editions of the Gita show the visarga rather than the actual letter that is to be chanted). e.g.

Anusvara ◌ं is pronounced as nasalized म् ।

In any case it is correct if Anusvara is pronounced as म् always. Anusvara will be reverted to म् at a pause or when it faces a vowel.

Reappearance of a dropped vowel

By an optional sandhi rule, the diphthong ए gets dropped. This will however be seen during a pause and uttered.

यक्ष्ये दास्यामि मोदिष्ये , इत्यज्ञानविमोहिताः ॥ 16.15

How to use this Book

To use this book effectively, listen to a chanting keeping the book open and notice the pauses. A couple of times listening to a Pandit or an audio CD is good enough to enable this book to be independently used thereafter.

The Sanskrit Alphabet

संस्कृत वर्णमाला

Sanskrit संस्कृत is written in the देवनागरी Devanagari script, whereas English is written in the Latin (Roman) script.

अ आ इ ई उ ऊ ऋ ॠ ऌ ॡ   ए ऐ ओ औ   अं अः   ॐ

					The Shiva Sounds
क	ख	ग	घ	ङ	
च	छ	ज	झ	ञ	
ट	ठ	ड	ढ	ण	The Brahma Sounds
त	थ	द	ध	न	
प	फ	ब	भ	म	The Vishnu Sounds
य र ल व		श ष स		ह	
		ळ	ळ्ह		Vedic Sanskrit
० १ २ ३ ४ ५ ६ ७ ८ ९					Numerals
क्ष ज्ञ श्र					Conjunct letter
Consonants are written with the vowel अ for enunciation					

The vowel long ॡ is not found in literature. It is given only in the alphabet, grammar books or in font sets. Hence crossed out.

Conjunct letter संयुक्त अक्षर

क्ष , ज्ञ , श्र are not letters of the alphabet. Rather these are conjuncts that have become popular in writing.

Alphabet as Commonly Written

The Sanskrit alphabet is written with or without a halant. Consonants cannot be uttered without a vowel. In teaching, consonants are supplied with vowel अ for uttering.

Here are the 56 letters of the Sanskrit Alphabet.

20 Vowels (ह्रस्व दीर्घ प्लुत short long hail)

अ आ अ३ इ ई इ३   उ ऊ उ३   ऋ ॠ ऋ३   ऌ ऌ३   ए ऐ ए३   ओ औ ओ३

34 Consonants (with halant the half-marker)

क्	ख्	ग्	घ्	ङ्
च्	छ्	ज्	झ्	ञ्
ट्	ठ्	ड्	ढ्	ण्
त्	थ्	द्	ध्	न्
प्	फ्	ब्	भ्	म्
य्	र्	ल्	व्	
श्	ष्	स्	ह्	
ळ्				

2 Ayogavahas (Anusvara, Visarga that appear during speaking)

अं   अः   (ardhavisarga अᵡ)

Notes:

- **Pluta Vowels** are rarely used in classical literature, but commonly used in Vedic texts.
- ळ is seen in Vedic texts.
- **Ardhavisarga** ◌ᵡ is seen in Vedic texts, but has become popular in chanting classical texts as well.

Pronunciation of Sanskrit Letters

उच्चारणम्

अ son	आ father	इ it	ई beat	उ full	ऊ pool
ऋ rhythm	ॠ marine	ऌ revelry	ॡ		
ए play	ऐ aisle	ओ go	औ loud		

अं Anusvara is pure nasal – close the lips – similar to म्

अः Visarga is Breath release like ह् and preceding vowel sound

E.g. utter नमः as नमह , शान्तिः as शान्तिहि , विष्णुः as विष्णुहु ।

क seek	ख khan	ग get	घ loghut	ङ sing
च chunk	छ catchhim	ज jump	झ hedgehog	ञ bunch
ट true	ठ anthill	ड drum	ढ godhead	ण under
त tamil	थ thunder	द that	ध breathe	न nut
प put	फ fruit	ब bin	भ abhor	म much
य loyal	र red	ल luck	व vase	
श sure	ष shun	स so	hum ह	

Conjuncts – first utter the top part and then bottom one,

e.g. Bhagavad Gita 10.16 तिष्ठसि → ष्ठ = ष् ठ

Bhagavad Gita 10.23 शङ्करश्चास्मि → ङ्क = ङ्क , श्च = श् च

Specific Conjuncts ह् ण = ह्ण , ह् न = ह्न , ह् म = ह्म

Utter with emphasis on the chest.

Place & Effort of Enunciation

Place of speech	Vowels स्वर		Row Consonants व्यञ्जन					Semi vowel	Sibilant
			Alpaprana		Mahaprana				
	Short	Long	1st	2nd	3rd	4th	5th		
throat	अ	आ	क्	ख्	ग्	घ्	ङ्		
palate	इ	ई	च्	छ्	ज्	झ्	ञ्	य्	श्
cerebral	ऋ	ॠ	ट्	ठ्	ड्	ढ्	ण्	र्	ष्
teeth	ऌ		त्	थ्	द्	ध्	न्	ल्	स्
lips	उ	ऊ	प्	फ्	ब्	भ्	म्		

कण्ठ – तालु	ए ऐ	**Diphthongs** = compound vowels have twin places of utterance
कण्ठ – ओष्ठ	ओ औ	
दन्त – ओष्ठ	व्	वकार is a special semivowel as it has twin places of utterance
नासिक्य	○ं , अं	Anusvara is a pure Nasal
अनुनासिका	○ँ , ॐ , यँ	**Candrabindu** = Nasalization
कण्ठ soft mahaprana	ह्	हकार is an Aspirate. It is sounded like a soft release of breath
	○:	Visarga is sounded like ह् along with its preceding vowel
कण्ठ hard alpaprana	○ᵡ + क्/ ख्	Ardhavisarga = Jihvamuliya utter as ह् = h
ओष्ठ hard alpaprana	○ᵡ + प् / फ्	Ardhavisarga = Upadhmaniya utter as फ् = f

कण्ठ्य	तालव्य	मूर्धन्य	दन्त्य	ओष्ठ्य
Guttural	Palatal	Cerebral	Dental	Labial

All vowels and semi vowels are termed voiced घोष वर्ण । This means that a background sound is produced from the tremor in the vocal cords in addition to the active sound produced in speaking. The 3rd, 4th and 5th letters of the row class consonants are also घोष वर्ण । The 1st and 2nd letters of the row class consonants, the sibilants and the aspirate are termed अघोष वर्ण । This means that no background sound arises from the tremor in the vocal cords. All row consonants are termed स्पर्शवर्ण i.e. Tongue makes contact.

Enunciation Time

- Unit of time for enunciation is a short vowel, 1 matra.
- Long vowels have 2 matras and are sounded twice as long as the short vowels.
- Diphthongs are combinations of two vowels सन्ध्यक्षर (सन्धि–अक्षर) having 2 matras and are sounded twice as long as the short vowels.
- A consonant has only ½ matra and it is supplied with a vowel for proper enunciation.
- Ardhavisarga is special with negligible vowel sound.

Pont of Contact of Tongue in the Mouth

GUTTURALS कण्ठ्य (also known as VELAR)

Sounded from the throat with the tongue resting.

PALATALS तालव्य (soft palate)

Sounded with the tongue raised slightly.

CEREBRALS मूर्धन्य (also RETROFLEX or LINGUAL, hard palate)

Sounded with tongue touching roof of mouth.

DENTALS दन्त्य

Sounded with the tongue distinctly touching the teeth.

LABIALS ओष्ठ्य

Sounded with the lips distinctly touching each other.

Tune of chanting the Bhagavad Gita

The Bhagavad Gita uses verses consisting of two sentences. Each sentence can be further divided in two so we have four quarters in each verse.

There are two tunes employed, the Anushtup consisting of eight syllables per quarter or 32 syllables per verse, and the Trishtup consisting of eleven syllables per quarter or 44 syllables per verse.

The anushtup meter has some variations while the trishtup meter has three variations depending upon which syllable is hrsva (h) or dirgha (d).

* Anushtup Meter अनुष्टुप् छन्दः 645/700 verses (8 syllabled) syllable syntax xxxxhddx xxxxhdhx xxxxhddx xxxxhdhx
* Trishtup Meter त्रिष्टुप् छन्दः 55/700 verses (11 syllabled)
    * Indravraja Meter इद्रव्रज छन्दः 3/700 verses 8.28, 15.5, 15.15 syllable syntax ddhd-dhhdhdd of each quarter
    * Upa Indravraja Meter उपेद्रव्रज छन्दः 3/700 verses 11.28, 11.29, 11.45 syllable syntax hdhd-dhhdhdd of each quarter
    * Upajati Meter उपजाति छन्दः 49/700 verses syllable syntax mix of Indravraja/Upendravraja of quarters
      Chapter 2: 5, 6, 7, 8, 20, 22, 29, 70
      Chapter 8: 9, 10, 11
      Chapter 9: 20, 21
      Chapter 11: 15-27, 30-44, 46-50
      Chapter 15: 2, 3, 4

Anushtup meter the main Tune

Meter or Chord or Tune अनुष्टुप् छन्दः

The Bhagavad Gita is written and sung in a definite meter known as the Anuṣṭup meter composed by Valmiki.

The rules of this chord are stated in this verse.
द्वात्रिंशद् अक्षर-अनुष्टुप् , चत्वारः अष्ट-अक्षरा गणाः ।
श्लोके षष्ठं गुरु ज्ञेयं , सर्वत्र लघु पञ्चमम् ।
द्विचतुःपादयोर्ह्स्वं सप्तमं , दीर्घम् अन्ययोः ॥

Translation

- The Anushtup meter consists of 32 syllables (distinct spoken sounds) in one verse, each verse contains 4 quarters (padas) of 8 syllables each.

- In each quarter the 6th syllable is dīrgha दीर्घः long, while the 5th syllable is hrsva ह्स्वः short.

- In the 2nd and 4th quarters, the 7th syllable is hrsva ह्स्वः , while in the remaining quarters it is dīrgha दीर्घः (i.e. 7th syllable in 1st and 3rd quarters is long).

In summary this means that a verse of 32 syllables should have 5th 6th 7th syllables as x = any, h = hrsva, d = dirgha.
12345678 ,12345678   12345678 , 12345678
xxxxhddx , xxxxhdhx I xxxxhddx , xxxxhdhx II

We find in gurukuls that while chanting the Bhagavad Gita, there is a definite pause at each quarter verse. We must also know the emphasized syllables during recitation.

Panini's Ashtadhyayi Rules for Hrsva Dirgha

1.2.27 ऊकालोऽज्झ्रस्वदीर्घप्लुतः ।

- Vowels similar to उ with 1 matra are called hrsva ह्रस्व
- Vowels similar to ऊ with 2 matra are called dirgha दीर्घ
- Vowels similar to उ with 3 matra are called pluta प्लुत

1.4.10 ह्रस्वं लघु ।

Hrsva ह्रस्व vowel is called laghu लघु also.

1.4.11 संयोगे गुरु ।

However when a ह्रस्व vowel is followed by a conjunct, it is

called गुरु guru.

1.4.12 दीर्घं च ।

And also a दीर्घ vowel is called गुरु guru.

Notes:

- Long vowels and diphthongs are दीर्घ dirgha. E.g. आ , ए
- Short vowels are ह्रस्व hrsva, e.g. अ , उ etc. But short vowels when followed by a conjunct are दीर्घ dirgha. E.g. अक्ष

Now we can apply the rules to the verses of the Bhagavad Gita to see its Anushtup meter.

Bhagavad Gita Chapter 1 Verse 1

धर्मक्षेत्रे कुरुक्षेत्रे समवेता युयुत्सवः ।

मामकाः पाण्डवाश्चैव किमकुर्वत सञ्जय ॥ १.१

Verse as chanted in Anushtup, pausing at each quarter

धर्मक्षेत्रे कुरुक्षेत्रे , समवेता युयुत्सवः ।

मामकाः पाण्डवाश्चैव , किमकुर्वत सञ्जय ॥ १.१

Quarter 1 धर्मक्षेत्रे कुरुक्षेत्रे The 5th 6th 7th Syllables

1	2	3	4	5	6	7	8
ध	र्म	क्षे	त्रे	कु	रु	क्षे	त्रे
				ह्रस्व	दीर्घ	दीर्घ	

Quarter 2 समवेता युयुत्सवः The 5th 6th 7th Syllables

1	2	3	4	5	6	7	8
स	म	वे	ता	यु	यु	त्स	वः
				ह्रस्व	दीर्घ	ह्रस्व	

Quarter 3 मामकाः पाण्डवाश्चैव The 5th 6th 7th Syllables

1	2	3	4	5	6	7	8
मा	म	काः	पा	ण्ड	वा	श्चै	व
				ह्रस्व	दीर्घ	दीर्घ	

Quarter 4 किमकुर्वत सञ्जय The 5th 6th 7th Syllables

1	2	3	4	5	6	7	8
कि	म	कु	र्व	त	स	ञ्ज	य
				ह्रस्व	दीर्घ	ह्रस्व	

Bhagavad Gita Chapter 1 Verse 9

अन्ये च बहवः शूरा मदर्थे त्यक्तजीविताः ।

नानाशस्त्रप्रहरणाः सर्वे युद्धविशारदाः ॥ १.९

Verse as chanted in Anushtup, pausing at each quarter

अन्ये च बहवश्शूराः , मदर्थे त्यक्तजीविताः ।

नानाशस्त्रप्रहरणाः , सर्वे युद्धविशारदाः ॥ १.९

Quarter 1 अन्ये च बहवश्शूराः The 5th 6th 7th Syllables

1	2	3	4	5	6	7	8
अ	न्ये	च	ब	ह	व	श्शू	राः
				ह्रस्व	दीर्घ	दीर्घ	

Quarter 2 मदर्थे त्यक्तजीविताः The 5th 6th 7th Syllables

1	2	3	4	5	6	7	8
म	द	र्थे	त्य	क्त	जी	वि	ताः
				ह्रस्व	दीर्घ	ह्रस्व	

Quarter 3 नानाशस्त्रप्रहरणाः The 5th 6th 7th Syllables

1	2	3	4	5	6	7	8
ना	ना	श	स्त्र	प्र	ह	र	णाः
				ह्रस्व	दीर्घ	दीर्घ	

Quarter 4 सर्वे युद्धविशारदाः The 5th 6th 7th Syllables

1	2	3	4	5	6	7	8
स	र्वे	यु	द्ध	वि	शा	र	दाः
				ह्रस्व	दीर्घ	ह्रस्व	

Bhagavad Gita Chapter 1 Verse 15

पाञ्चजन्यं हृषीकेशो देवदत्तं धनञ्जयः ।

पौण्ड्रं दध्मौ महाशङ्खं भीमकर्मा वृकोदरः ॥ १.१५

Verse as chanted in Anushtup, pausing at each quarter

पाञ्चजन्यं हृषीकेशः , देवदत्तं धनञ्जयः ।

पौण्ड्रं दध्मौ महाशङ्खं , भीमकर्मा वृकोदरः ॥ १.१५

Quarter 1 पाञ्चजन्यं हृषीकेशः The 5th 6th 7th Syllables

1	2	3	4	5	6	7	8
पा	ञ्च	ज	न्यं	ह	षी	के	शः
				ह्रस्व	दीर्घ	दीर्घ	

Quarter 2 देवदत्तं धनञ्जयः The 5th 6th 7th Syllables

1	2	3	4	5	6	7	8
दे	व	द	त्तं	ध	न	ञ्ज	यः
				ह्रस्व	दीर्घ	ह्रस्व	

Quarter 3 पौण्ड्रं दध्मौ महाशङ्खं The 5th 6th 7th Syllables

1	2	3	4	5	6	7	8
पौ	ण्ड्रं	द	ध्मौ	म	हा	श	ङ्खं
				ह्रस्व	दीर्घ	दीर्घ	

Quarter 4 भीमकर्मा वृकोदरः The 5th 6th 7th Syllables

1	2	3	4	5	6	7	8
भी	म	क	र्मा	वृ	को	द	रः
				ह्रस्व	दीर्घ	ह्रस्व	

Bhagavad Gita Chapter 2 Verse 50

बुद्धियुक्तो जहातीह उभे सुकृतदुष्कृते ।

तस्माद्योगाय युज्यस्व योगः कर्मसु कौशलम् ॥ २.५०

Verse as chanted in Anushtup, pausing at each quarter

बुद्धियुक्तो जहातीह , उभे सुकृतदुष्कृते ।

तस्माद्योगाय युज्यस्व , योगः कर्मसु कौशलम् ॥ २.५०

Quarter 1 बुद्धियुक्तो जहातीह The 5th 6th 7th Syllables

1	2	3	4	5	6	7	8
बु	द्धि	यु	क्तो	ज	हा	ती	ह
				ह्रस्व	दीर्घ	दीर्घ	

Quarter 2 उभे सुकृतदुष्कृते The 5th 6th 7th Syllables

1	2	3	4	5	6	7	8
उ	भे	सु	कृ	त	दु	ष्कृ	ते
				ह्रस्व	दीर्घ	ह्रस्व	

Quarter 3 तस्माद्योगाय युज्यस्व The 5th 6th 7th Syllables

1	2	3	4	5	6	7	8
त	स्मा	द्यो	गा	य	यु	ज्य	स्व
				ह्रस्व	दीर्घ	दीर्घ	

Quarter 4 योगः कर्मसु कौशलम् The 5th 6th 7th Syllables

1	2	3	4	5	6	7	8
यो	गः	क	र्म	सु	कौ	श	लम्
				ह्रस्व	दीर्घ	ह्रस्व	

Bhagavad Gita Chapter 2 Verse 55

प्रजहाति यदा कामान्सर्वान्पार्थ मनोगतान् ।

आत्मन्येवात्मना तुष्ः स्थितप्रज्ञस्तदोच्यते ॥ २.५५

Verse as chanted in Anushtup, pausing at each quarter

प्रजहाति यदा कामान् , सर्वान्पार्थ मनोगतान् ।

आत्मन्येवात्मना तुष्ः , स्थितप्रज्ञस्तदोच्यते ॥ २.५५

Quarter 1 प्रजहाति यदा कामान् The 5th 6th 7th Syllables

1	2	3	4	5	6	7	8
प्र	ज	हा	ति	य	दा	का	मान्
				ह्रस्व	दीर्घ	दीर्घ	

Quarter 2 सर्वान्पार्थ मनोगतान् The 5th 6th 7th Syllables

1	2	3	4	5	6	7	8
स	र्वा	न्या	र्थ	म	नो	ग	तान्
				ह्रस्व	दीर्घ	ह्रस्व	

Quarter 3 आत्मन्येवात्मना तुष्ः The 5th 6th 7th Syllables

1	2	3	4	5	6	7	8
आ	त्म	न्ये	वा	त्म	ना	तु	ष्ः
				ह्रस्व	दीर्घ	दीर्घ	

Quarter 4 स्थितप्रज्ञस्तदोच्यते The 5th 6th 7th Syllables

1	2	3	4	5	6	7	8
स्थि	त	प्र	ज्ञ	स्त	दो	च्य	ते
				ह्रस्व	दीर्घ	ह्रस्व	

Bhagavad Gita Chapter 4 Verse 7

यदा यदा हि धर्मस्य ग्लानिर्भवति भारत ।

अभ्युत्थानमधर्मस्य तदाऽऽत्मानं सृजाम्यहम् ॥ ४.७

Verse as chanted in Anushtup, pausing at each quarter

यदा यदा हि धर्मस्य , ग्लानिर्भवति भारत ।

अभ्युत्थानमधर्मस्य , तदात्मानं सृजाम्यहम् ॥ ४.७

Quarter 1 यदा यदा हि धर्मस्य The 5th 6th 7th Syllables

1	2	3	4	5	6	7	8
य	दा	य	दा	हि	ध	र्म	स्य
				ह्रस्व	दीर्घ	दीर्घ	

Quarter 2 ग्लानिर्भवति भारत The 5th 6th 7th Syllables

1	2	3	4	5	6	7	8
ग्ला	नि	र्भ	व	ति	भा	र	त
				ह्रस्व	दीर्घ	ह्रस्व	

Quarter 3 अभ्युत्थानमधर्मस्य The 5th 6th 7th Syllables

1	2	3	4	5	6	7	8
अ	भ्यु	त्था	न	म	ध	र्म	स्य
				ह्रस्व	दीर्घ	दीर्घ	

Quarter 4 तदात्मानं सृजाम्यहम् The 5th 6th 7th Syllables

1	2	3	4	5	6	7	8
त	दा	त्मा	नं	सृ	जा	म्य	हम्
				ह्रस्व	दीर्घ	ह्रस्व	

Bhagavad Gita Chapter 4 Verse 24

ब्रह्मार्पणं ब्रह्महविर्ब्रह्माग्नौ ब्रह्मणा हुतम् ।

ब्रह्मैव तेन गन्तव्यं ब्रह्मकर्मसमाधिना ॥ ४.२४

Verse as chanted in Anushtup, pausing at each quarter

ब्रह्मार्पणं ब्रह्महविः , ब्रह्माग्नौ ब्रह्मणा हुतम् ।

ब्रह्मैव तेन गन्तव्यं , ब्रह्मकर्मसमाधिना ॥ ४.२४

Quarter 1 ब्रह्मार्पणं ब्रह्महविः The 5th 6th 7th Syllables

1	2	3	4	5	6	7	8
ब्र	ह्मा	र्प	णं	ब्र	ह्म	ह	विः
				ह्रस्व	दीर्घ	दीर्घ	

Quarter 2 ब्रह्माग्नौ ब्रह्मणा हुतम् The 5th 6th 7th Syllables

1	2	3	4	5	6	7	8
ब्र	ह्मा	ग्नौ	ब्र	ह्म	णा	हु	तम्
				ह्रस्व	दीर्घ	ह्रस्व	

Quarter 3 ब्रह्मैव तेन गन्तव्यं The 5th 6th 7th Syllables

1	2	3	4	5	6	7	8
ब्र	ह्मै	व	ते	न	ग	न्त	व्यं
				ह्रस्व	दीर्घ	दीर्घ	

Quarter 4 ब्रह्मकर्मसमाधिना The 5th 6th 7th Syllables

1	2	3	4	5	6	7	8
ब्र	ह्म	क	र्म	स	मा	धि	ना
				ह्रस्व	दीर्घ	ह्रस्व	

Bhagavad Gita Chapter 15 Verse 5 (Trishtup Indravraja Meter)

निर्मानमोहा जितसङ्गदोषा अध्यात्मनित्या विनिवृत्तकामाः ।

द्वन्द्वैर् विमुक्तास् सुखदुःखसञ्ज्ञैर्गच्छन्त्यमूढाः पदमव्ययं तत् ॥ १५.५

Verse as chanted in Trishtup, pausing at each quarter

निर्मानमोहा जितसङ्गदोषाः , अध्यात्मनित्या विनिवृत्तकामाः ।

द्वन्द्वैर् विमुक्तास् सुखदुःखसञ्ज्ञैः , गच्छन्त्यमूढाः पदमव्ययं तत् ॥ १५.५

Quarter 1 निर्मानमोहा जितसङ्गदोषाः

1	2	3	4	5	6	7	8	9	10	11
नि	र्मा	न	मो	हा	जि	त	स	ङ्ग	दो	षाः
d	d	h	d	d	h	h	d	h	d	d

Quarter 2 अध्यात्मनित्या विनिवृत्तकामाः

1	2	3	4	5	6	7	8	9	10	11
अ	ध्या	त्म	नि	त्या	वि	नि	वृ	त्त	का	माः
d	d	h	d	d	h	h	d	h	d	d

Quarter 3 द्वन्द्वैर्विमुक्तास्सुखदुःखसञ्ज्ञैः

1	2	3	4	5	6	7	8	9	10	11
द्व	न्द्वै	वि	मु	क्ता	स्सु	ख	दुः	ख	स	ञ्ज्ञैः
d	d	h	d	d	h	h	d	h	d	d

Quarter 4 गच्छन्त्यमूढाः पदमव्ययं तत्

1	2	3	4	5	6	7	8	9	10	11
ग	च्छ	न्त्य	मू	ढाः	प	द	म	व्य	यं	तत्
d	d	h	d	d	h	h	d	h	d	d

Bhagavad Gita Chapter 18 Verse 66

सर्वधर्मान्परित्यज्य मामेकं शरणं व्रज ।

अहं त्वा सर्वपापेभ्यो मोक्षयिष्यामि मा शुचः ॥ १८.६६

Verse as chanted in Anushtup, pausing at each quarter

सर्वधर्मान् परित्यज्य , मामेकं शरणं व्रज ।

अहं त्वा सर्वपापेभ्यः , मोक्षयिष्यामि मा शुचः ॥ १८.६६

Quarter 1 सर्वधर्मान् परित्यज्य The 5th 6th 7th Syllables

1	2	3	4	5	6	7	8
स	र्व	ध	र्मा	न्प	रि	त्य	ज्य
				ह्रस्व	दीर्घ	दीर्घ	

Quarter 2 मामेकं शरणं व्रज The 5th 6th 7th Syllables

1	2	3	4	5	6	7	8
मा	मे	कं	श	र	णं	व्र	ज
				ह्रस्व	दीर्घ	ह्रस्व	

Quarter 3 अहं त्वा सर्वपापेभ्यः The 5th 6th 7th Syllables

1	2	3	4	5	6	7	8
अ	हं	त्वा	स	र्व	पा	पे	भ्यः
				ह्रस्व	दीर्घ	दीर्घ	

Quarter 4 मोक्षयिष्यामि मा शुचः The 5th 6th 7th Syllables

1	2	3	4	5	6	7	8
मो	क्ष	यि	ष्या	मि	मा	शु	चः
				ह्रस्व	दीर्घ	ह्रस्व	

Sample Verses Recitation Notes

We have selected specific verses that highlight all the nuances during chanting. Using these as a guide, we can then apply the same chanting method to all the other similar verses in the Bhagavad Gita.

1.1 dharmakṣetre kurukṣetre , samavetā yuyutsavaḥ ।

māmakāḥ pāṇḍavāścaiva , kimakurvata sañjaya ॥

धर्मक्षेत्रे कुरुक्षेत्रे , समवेता युयुत्सवः । मामकाः पाण्डवाश्चैव , किमकुर्वत सञ्जय ॥

Visarga facing a pause वः + । → वह ।

Visarga to Ardhavisarga काः + प् → का× + प्

Visarga to शकार, वाः + च् → वाश् + च् → वाश्च

Anusvara to Nasal सं + ज् → सञ्ज

1.7 asmākaṃ tu viśiṣṭā ye , tānnibodha dvijottama ।

nāyakā mama sainyasya , sañjñārthaṃ tānbravīmi te ॥

अस्माकं तु विशिष्टा ये , तान्निबोध द्विजोत्तम ।

नायका मम सैन्यस्य , सञ्ज्ञार्थं तान्ब्रवीमि ते ॥

Anusvara to Nasal कं + तु → कन् + तु

1.9 anye ca bahavaḥ śūrā , madarthe tyaktajīvitāḥ ।

nānāśastrapraharaṇāḥ , sarve yuddhaviśāradāḥ ॥

अन्ये च बहवः शूरा , मदर्थे त्यक्तजीविताः ।

नानाशस्त्रप्रहरणाः , सर्वे युद्धविशारदाः ॥

Visarga to शकार, वः + श् → वश् + श् → वश्श्

Reappearance of Visarga facing a pause रा + , → राः + , → राहा ,

Visarga facing a pause ताः + । → ताहा । Similarly णाहा दाहा

1.15 pāñcajanyaṃ hṛṣīkeśo , devadattaṃ dhanañjayaḥ |
pauṇḍraṃ dadhmau mahāśaṅkham , bhīmakarmā vṛkodaraḥ ||

पाञ्चजन्यं हृषीकेशो, देवदत्तं धनञ्जयः। पौण्ड्रं दध्मौ महाशङ्खं, भीमकर्मा वृकोदरः ॥

Anusvara to Nasal पां + च् → पाञ्च

Reappearance of Visarga facing a pause शो + , → शः + , → शह ,

Anusvara to Nasal नं + ज् → नञ्ज

Anusvara to Nasal शं + ख् → शङ्ख

Anusvara to मकार facing a pause खं + , → खम् + ,

Visarga facing a pause रः + || → रह ||

2.32 yadṛcchayā copapannam , svargadvāram apāvṛtam |
sukhinaḥ kṣatriyāꓘ pārtha , labhante yuddhamīdṛśam ||

यदृच्छया चोपपन्नम् , स्वर्गद्वारम् अपावृतम् ।
सुखिनः क्षत्रियाꓘ पार्थ , लभन्ते युद्धमीदृशम् ॥

Visarga facing a क्ष = क् ष् remains as it is (without changing to ardhavisarga).

2.50 buddhiyukto jahātīha , ubhe sukṛtaduṣkṛte |
tasmādyogāya yujyasva , yogaḥ karmasu kauśalam ||

बुद्धियुक्तो जहातीह , उभे सुकृतदुष्कृते ।
तस्माद्योगाय युज्यस्व , योगः कर्मसु कौशलम् ॥

Visarga to ओकार, क्तः + ज् → क्तो + ज्

Visarga to Ardhavisarga गः + क् → गꓘ + क्

2.55 prajahāti yadā kāmān , sarvānpārtha manogatān |

ātmanyevātmanā tuṣṭah , sthitaprajñastadocyate ||

प्रजहाति यदा कामान् , सर्वान्पार्थ मनोगतान् ।

आत्मन्येवात्मना तुष्टः , स्थितप्रज्ञस्तदोच्यते ॥

Visarga facing a pause ए: + , → एह ,

Visarga to सकार, ज्ञः + त् → ज्ञस् + त् → ज्ञस्त्

4.7 yadā hi dharmasya , glānirbhavati bhārata |

abhyutthānamadharmasya , tadā"tmānaṃ sṛjāmyaham ||

यदा यदा हि धर्मस्य , ग्लानिर्भवति भारत ।

अभ्युत्थानमधर्मस्य , तदाऽऽत्मानं सृजाम्यहम् ॥

Visarga to रेफ, निः + भ् → निर् + भ् → निर्भ्

Avagraha is a silent letter दा + आ → दा + ऽऽ → दाऽऽ → दा

4.24 brahmārpaṇaṃ brahmahavirbrahmāgnau brahmaṇā hutam |

brahmaiva tena gantavyaṃ brahmakarmasamādhinā ||

ब्रह्मार्पणं ब्रह्महविर्ब्रह्माग्नौ ब्रह्मणा हुतम् । ब्रह्मैव तेन गन्तव्यं ब्रह्मकर्मसमाधिना ॥

Visarga to रेफ, विः + ब् → विर् + ब् → विर्ब्

Anusvara to Nasal गं + त् → न्त्

15.5 nirmānamohā jitasaṅgadoṣāḥ ,
adhyātmanityā vinivṛttakāmāḥ |
dvandvair vimuktās sukhaduḥkhasañjñaiḥ ,
gacchantyamūḍhāx padam avyayaṃ tat ‖ Trishtup

निर्मानमोहा जितसङ्गदोषाः ,

अध्यात्मनित्या विनिवृत्तकामाः ।

द्वन्द्वैर् विमुक्तास् सुखदुःखसञ्ज्ञैः ,

गच्छन्त्यमूढाx पदम् अव्ययं तत् ‖ **Trishtup Chhand Verse**
Visarga facing a pause

Sample Verses Recited

1 Yoga of Meeting Oneself

ॐ श्री परमात्मने नमः । अथ प्रथमोऽध्यायः

1.1 Verse as written, with sandhis and conjuncts together

धृतराष्ट्र उवाच

धर्मक्षेत्रे कुरुक्षेत्रे समवेता युयुत्सवः ।

मामकाः पाण्डवाश्चैव किमकुर्वत सञ्जय ॥ १.१

Verse as chanted, pausing at each pada i.e. Quarter verse

धृतराष्ट्र उवाच	See each letter and syllable clearly
धर्मक्षेत्रे कुरुक्षेत्रे ,	धर्म-क्षेत्रे कुरु-क्षेत्रे ,
समवेता युयुत्सवः ।	सम-वेता युयुत्-सवः ।
मामकाꣳ पाण्डवाश्चैव ,	मामकाꣳ पाण्ड-वाश्-चैव ,
किमकुर्वत सञ्जय ॥ १.१	किम-कुर्वत सञ्जय ॥ १.१

Chanting Notes

सवः ।

Here the visarga is immediately followed by a pause. Hence it is to be enunciated as हकार along with sound of previous vowel, in this case अकार । So chant the visarga as ह्+अ = ह → सवह ।

मामकाꣳ पा

Here the visarga is immediately followed by a प् / फ् । Hence it is to be enunciated as फकार । So chant the visarga as फ् → मामकाफ् पा

पाण्डवाश् चै

Here the visarga is immediately followed by a च् / श् । Hence it is to be enunciated as शकार । So chant the visarga as श् । *Same as written.*

1.9 Verse as written, with sandhis and conjuncts together

अन्ये च बहवः शूरा मदर्थे त्यक्तजीविताः ।

नानाशस्त्रप्रहरणाः सर्वे युद्धविशारदाः ॥ १.९

Verse as chanted, pausing at each pada i.e. Quarter verse

अन्ये च बहवश्शूराः ,	अन्ये च बहवश् शूराः ,
मदर्थे त्यक्तजीविताः ।	मदर्थे त्यक्त-जीविताः ।
नानाशस्त्रप्रहरणाः ,	नाना-शस्त्र-प्रहरणाः ,
सर्वे युद्धविशारदाः ॥ १.९	सर्वे युद्ध-विशारदाः ॥ १.९

Chanting Notes

बहवः शूरा → बहवश् शूरा → बहवश्शूरा

Here the visarga is immediately followed by a च / श । By Sandhi it is to be enunciated as शकार । *Same as written.*

शूराः ,

Here the visarga is immediately followed by a pause. Hence it is to be enunciated as हकार along with sound of previous vowel, in this case आकार । So chant the visarga as हू+आ = हा →

शूराहा ,

Note - written verse has शूरा dropped visarga due to Sandhi.

Similarly त्यक्तजीविताः । → त्यक्तजीविताहा ।

नानाशस्त्रप्रहरणाः , → नानाशस्त्रप्रहरणाहा ,

युद्धविशारदाः ॥ → युद्धविशारदाहा ॥

1.15 Verse as written, with sandhis and conjuncts together

पाञ्चजन्यं हृषीकेशो देवदत्तं धनञ्जयः ।

पौण्ड्रं दध्मौ महाशङ्खं भीमकर्मा वृकोदरः ॥ १.१५

Verse as chanted, pausing at each pada i.e. Quarter verse

पाञ्चजन्यं हृषीकेशः , देवदत्तं धनञ्जयः । पौण्ड्रं दध्मौ महाशङ्खम् , भीमकर्मा वृकोदरः ॥ १.१५	पाञ्च-जन्यं हृषी-केशः , देव-दत्तं धनञ्-जयः । पौण्ड्रं दध्मौ महा-शङ्-खम् , भीम-कर्मा वृकोदरः ॥ १.१५

Chanting Notes

हृषीकेशः ,

Here the written verse has हृषीकेशो , wherein a visarga has changed to ओकार due to sandhi. However for chanting, we see that visarga is immediately followed by a **pause**. Hence it is to be enunciated as हकार along with sound of previous vowel, in this case अकार । So chant the visarga as ह्+अ = ह → हृषीकेशह ,

2 Yoga of Meeting The Lord

ॐ श्री परमात्मने नमः । अथ द्वितीयोऽध्यायः

2.50 Verse as written, with sandhis and conjuncts together
बुद्धियुक्तो जहातीह उभे सुकृतदुष्कृते ।
तस्माद्योगाय युज्यस्व योगः कर्मसु कौशलम् ॥ २.५०

Verse as chanted, pausing at each pada i.e. Quarter verse

बुद्धियुक्तो जहातीह , उभे सुकृतदुष्कृते । तस्माद्योगाय युज्यस्व , योगः कर्मसु कौशलम् ॥ २.५०	बुद्धि-युक्तो जहा-तीह , उभे सुकृत-दुष्कृते । तस्माद्-योगाय युज्-यस्व , योगः कर्मसु कौशलम् ॥ २.५०

Chanting Notes

बुद्धियुक्तः ज → बुद्धियुक्तो ज

Here the written verse has बुद्धियुक्तो , wherein a visarga has changed to ओकार due to sandhi. *Same for chanting.*

योगः क → योग॒ क

Here the visarga is immediately followed by a क् / ख् । Hence it is to be enunciated as हकार । So chant the visarga as हू →
योगहू क

2.55 Verse as written, with sandhis and conjuncts together
श्री भगवानुवाच
प्रजहाति यदा कामान्सर्वान्पार्थ मनोगतान् ।
आत्मन्येवात्मना तुष्टः स्थितप्रज्ञस्तदोच्यते ॥ २.५५
Verse as chanted, pausing at each pada i.e. Quarter verse
श्री भगवान् उवाच

प्रजहाति यदा कामान् ,	प्रज-हाति यदा कामान् ,
सर्वान्पार्थ मनोगतान् ।	सर्वान्-पार्थ मनो-गतान् ।
आत्मन्येवात्मना तुष्टः ,	आत्-मन्ये-वात्-मना तुष्टः ,
स्थितप्रज्ञस्तदोच्यते ॥ २.५५	स्थित-प्रज्ञस्-तदोच्यते ॥ २.५५

Chanting Notes

स्थितप्रज्ञः तदोच्यते → स्थितप्रज्ञस् तदोच्यते → स्थितप्रज्ञस्तदोच्यते
Here the written verse has स्थितप्रज्ञस्तदोच्यते, wherein a visarga has changed to सकार due to sandhi. *Same for chanting.*

तुष्टः स्थितप्रज्ञस्तदोच्यते → तुष्टः , स्थितप्रज्ञस्तदोच्यते
Here even though the visarga is followed by a सकार , it does not change, since there is a pause तुष्टः , during chanting.

4 Yoga of Intention

ॐ श्री परमात्मने नमः । अथ चतुर्थोऽध्यायः

4.7 Verse as written, with sandhis and conjuncts together

यदा यदा हि धर्मस्य ग्लानिर्भवति भारत ।

अभ्युत्थानमधर्मस्य तदाऽऽत्मानं सृजाम्यहम् ॥ ४.७

Verse as chanted, pausing at each pada i.e. Quarter verse

यदा यदा हि धर्मस्य ,	यदा यदा हि धर्-मस्य ,
ग्लानिर्भवति भारत ।	ग्लानिर्-भवति भारत ।
अभ्युत्थानम् अधर्मस्य ,	अभ्युत्-थानम् अधर्मस्य ,
तदात्मानं सृजाम्यहम् ॥ ४.७	तदात्-मानं सृजाम्य-हम् ॥ ४.७

Chanting Notes

ग्लानिः भवति → ग्लानिर् भवति → ग्लानिर्भवति

Here the written verse has ग्लानिर्भवति, wherein a visarga has changed to रेफ due to sandhi. *Same for chanting.*

4.24 Verse as written, with sandhis and conjuncts together

ब्रह्मार्पणं ब्रह्महविर्ब्रह्माग्नौ ब्रह्मणा हुतम् ।

ब्रह्मैव तेन गन्तव्यं ब्रह्मकर्मसमाधिना ॥ ४.२४

Verse as chanted, pausing at each pada i.e. Quarter verse

ब्रह्मार्पणं ब्रह्म हविः ,	ब्रह्मार्-पणं ब्रह्म हविः ,
ब्रह्माग्नौ ब्रह्मणा हुतम् ।	ब्रह्म-आग्नौ ब्रह्मणा हुतम् ।
ब्रह्मैव तेन गन्तव्यम् ,	ब्रह्मैव तेन गन्-तव्यम् ,
ब्रह्मकर्मसमाधिना ॥ ४.२४	ब्रह्म-कर्म-समाधिना ॥ ४.२४

Chanting Notes

ब्रह्महविर्ब्रह्माग्नौ → ब्रह्महविः , ब्रह्माग्नौ

ब्रह्महवि: ,

Here the visarga is immediately followed by a pause. Hence it is to be enunciated as हकार along with sound of previous vowel, in this case इकार । So chant the visarga as हू+इ = हि → ब्रह्महविहि ,

18 Yoga of Liberation

ॐ श्री परमात्मने नमः ।   अथ अष्टादशोऽध्यायः

18.66 Verse as written, with sandhis and conjuncts together

सर्वधर्मान्परित्यज्य मामेकं शरणं व्रज ।

अहं त्वा सर्वपापेभ्यो मोक्षयिष्यामि मा शुचः ॥ १८.६६

Verse as chanted, pausing at each pada i.e. Quarter verse

सर्वधर्मान्परित्यज्य ,	सर्व-धर्मान् परि-त्यज्य ,
मामेकं शरणं व्रज ।	मामेकं शरणं व्रज ।
अहं त्वा सर्वपापेभ्यः ,	अहं त्वा सर्व-पापे-भ्यः ,
मोक्षयिष्यामि मा शुचः ॥ १८.६६	मोक्ष-यिष्-यामि मा शुचः ॥ १८.६६

Panini's Ashtadhyayi Rules for Consonant Sandhi

A few sandhi rules are given, those that help differentiate between Bhagavad Gita as recited vs as written.

जश् त्वम्

8.2.39 झलां जशोऽन्ते ।

The झल् letter at the end of a word is replaced by a corresponding जश् letter.

Definition of झल् letter = Maheshwar Sutras 8, 9, 10, 11, 12, 13, 14 = 1st 2nd 3rd 4th letters of class consonants and sibilants श् ष् स् and aspirate ह् ।

Definition of जश् letter = Maheshwar Sutra 10 = 3rd letter of each class consonant = ग् ज् ड् द् ब् ।

श्चु त्वम्

8.4.40 स्तोः श्चुना श्चुः ।

The स् facing a श् changes to श् ।

The स् facing a चवर्ग letter changes to श् ।

The तवर्ग letter facing a श् changes to corresponding चवर्ग ।

The तवर्ग letter facing चवर्ग letter changes to corresponding चवर्ग ।

e.g. verse 4.33 यज्ञात् ज्ञानयज्ञः → 8.2.39 → यज्ञाध् ज्ञानयज्ञः → यज्ञाध् ज् ञ् आनयज्ञः → 8.4.40 → यज्ञाज् ज् ञ् आनयज्ञः → यज्ञाज् ज्ञानयज्ञः → यज्ञाज्ज्ञानयज्ञः as written. However for recitation, there is a pause

यज्ञात् , ज्ञानयज्ञः as recited.

चर् त्वम्

8.4.55 खरि च ।

The झल् letter when followed by a खर् letter is replaced by a corresponding चर् letter. The sibilants will be replaced by themselves.

Definition of झल् letter – Maheshvarani Sutrani 8 9 10 11 12 13 14 = 1st 2nd 3rd 4th letters of class consonants and sibilants श् ष् स् and aspirate ह् । *ह् is not considered here because it undergoes other sandhis.*

Definition of चर् letter – Maheshvarani Sutrani 11, 12, 13 – all are hard consonants = The 1st letter of each class consonant क् च् ट् त् प् and sibilants श् ष् स् ।

Definition of खर् letter – Maheshvarani Sutrani 11, 12, 13 – all are hard consonants = The 1st and 2nd letters of each class consonant क् ख् च् छ् ट् ठ् त् थ् प् फ् and sibilants श् ष् स् ।

e.g. verse 5.4 सम्यक् उभयोर्विन्दते → 8.2.39 → सम्यग् उभयोर्विन्दते → सम्यगुभयोर्विन्दते as written. However during recitation there is a pause सम्यग् , → 8.4.56 → सम्यक् , as recited.

8.4.56 वाऽवसाने ।

The झल् letter facing a pause or fullstop is replaced by a corresponding चर् letter, Optionally.

Definition of झल् letter – Maheshvarani Sutrani 8 9 10 11 12 13 14 = 1st 2nd 3rd 4th letters of all class consonants and sibilants श् ष् स् and aspirate ह् । *Note – श् , ष् , स्, and ह् are not considered here because they undergo other sandhis.*

Definition of जश् letter – Maheshvarani Sutrani 10 = The 3rd letter of each class consonant = ग् ज् ड् द् ब् ।

Definition of चर् letter – Maheshvarani Sutrani 11, 12, 13 = The 1st letter of each class consonant and sibilants = क् च् ट् त् प् , श् ष् स् ।

e.g. verse 5.4 सम्यक् उभयोर्विन्दते → 8.2.39 → सम्यग् उभयोर्विन्दते → सम्यगुभयोर्विन्दते as written. However during recitation there is a pause सम्यग् , → 8.4.56 → सम्यक् , as recited.

ङम् आगम त्वम्

8.3.32 ङमो ह्रस्वादचि ङमुण्णित्यम् ।

When the nasals ङ् , ण् , न् are preceded by a ह्रस्व-vowel and are followed by any vowel, then these nasals are doubled. Precisely, the ह्रस्व-vowel gets a ङम् आगमः ।

Definition of ङम् letters – Maheshwar Sutra 7 = ङ् ण् न् i.e. the guttural, cerebral and dental nasals.

e.g. verse 5.8 जिघ्रन् अश्नन् → 8.3.32 → जिघ्रन्न् अश्नन् → जिघ्रन्नश्नन् as written. However during recitation there is a pause जिघ्रन् , अश्नन् as recited.

e.g. verse 5.9 गृह्ण्नुन्मिषन् as written. However during recitation there is a pause गृह्ण् , उन्मिषन् as recited.

नश्छव्य् त्वम्

8.3.7 नश्छव्य् अप्रशान् ।

When a पदान्त न् is followed by छव् letter that itself is followed by अम् letter, then the न् is replaced by रुँ , except for word प्रशान् ।

8.3.2 अत्रानुनासिकः पूर्वस्य तु वा ।

The letter preceding (that letter for which रुँ has been substituted), is replaced by a nasal vowel, Optionally.

1.3.2 उपदेशेऽजनुनासिक इत् ।

In this grammar, a nasalized letter is a Tag.

Definition of छव् letter – Maheshwar Sutra 11 = छ ठ् थ् च् ट् त्

i.e. the hard palatal, cerebral and dental consonants.

Definition of अम् letter – Maheshwar Sutras 1 2 3 4 5 6 7

i.e. all vowels, semivowels, nasals, aspirate = अ आ इ ई उ ऊ ऋ ॠ ऌ ए ऐ ओ औ , य् र् ल् व् , ङ् ञ् ण न म् , ह् ।

e.g. verse 5.27 बाह्यान् चक्षुः → बाह्यान् च् अ क्षुः → 8.3.7 → बाह्यारुँ चक्षुः → 8.3.2 + 8.3.4 → बाह्य् आं रुँ चक्षुः → बाह्यांरुँ चक्षुः → 1.3.2 → बाह्यांर् चक्षुः → 8.3.15 → बाह्यां ः चक्षुः → 8.3.34 + 8.4.40 बाह्यां श् चक्षुः → बाह्यांश्चक्षुः as written. However during recitation there is a pause बाह्यान् , चक्षुः as recited.

e.g. verse 6.24 कामांस्त्यक्त्वा as written. However during recitation there is a pause कामान् , त्यक्त्वा as recited.

सुँ लोप त्वम्

6.1.132 एतत्तदोः सुलोपोऽकोरनञ्समासे हलि ।

For the words एषः and सः made by the 1st case singular vibhakti सुँ , this vibhakti सुँ is dropped when any consonant follows.

e.g. verse 3.37 एष रजोगुणसमुद्भवः as written. However during recitation there is a pause एषः , रजोगुणसमुद्भवः as recited.

एच् लोप त्वम्

6.1.78 एचोऽयवायावः ।

When vowel एच् (ए ऐ ओ औ) is followed by अच् any vowel, then it are replaced by अय् आय् अव् आव् respectively. By extrapolation we add to it अर् आर् अल् ।

Definition of एच् letter – Maheshwar Sutras 3 and 4 = ए ऐ ओ औ

Definition of अच् letter – Maheshwar Sutras 1 2 3 and 4 = all vowels अ आ इ ई उ ऊ ऋ ॠ ऌ ए ऐ ओ औ

8.3.19 लोपः शाकल्यस्य ।

पदान्त य् or व् when preceded by अवर्ण and followed by अश् is dropped, Optionally. There is no further Sandhi. Usually seen after अयाव् sandhi.

e.g. verse 16.15 मोदिष्ये इत्यज्ञानविमोहिताः → मोदिष्य् ए इत्यज्ञानविमोहिताः → 8.3.7 → मोदिष्य् अय् इत्यज्ञानविमोहिताः → मोदिष्यय् इत्यज्ञानविमोहिताः → 8.3.19 → मोदिष्य इत्यज्ञानविमोहिताः as written. However during recitation there is a pause मोदिष्ये , इत्यज्ञानविमोहिताः as recited.

अनुनासिक त्वम्

8.4.45 यरोऽनुनासिकेऽनुनासिको वा ।

A पदान्त यर् letter followed by ञम् nasal consonant is optionally replaced by the nasal of its own class.

Definition of यर् = all consonants, except ह् aspirate.

Definition of ञम् = all nasals = ङ् ञ् ण् न् म्

e.g. verse 10.39 स्यात् मया → 8.4.45 → स्यान् मया → स्यान्मया as written. However during recitation there is a pause स्यात् , मया as recited.

तोर्लि त्वम्

8.4.60 तोर्लि ।

A consonant of तवर्ग followed by ल् is replaced by one

homogenous with the latter. By this Sandhi, तकार facing लकार

gets replaced by लकार, as both त् ल् are dental consonants, hence homogenous.

e.g. verse 11.30 समन्तात् लोकान् → 8.4.60 → समन्ताल् लोकान् → समन्ताल्लोकान् as written. However during recitation there is a pause समन्तात् , लोकान् as recited.

Panini's Ashtadhyayi Rules for Visarga

Visarga ॰: results from final (पदान्त) र् or स् ।

8.2.66 ससजुषोः रुँ ।

Appearance of रुँ from सकार ।

- Final स् of any word changes to रुँ → र्
- Final ष् of the word सजुष् changes to रुँ → र्

8.3.15 खर् अवसानयोः विसर्जनीयः ।

Appearance of Visarga.

- When a Final repha र् is followed by खर् hard consonant or a sibilant, Visarga appears in place of repha.
- When a Final repha र् is followed by Virama (pause), Visarga appears in place of repha.

Definition of खर् – 1st 2nd letters of the class consonants क् ख् च् छ् ट् ठ् त् थ् प् फ् which are hard consonants, श् ष् स् sibilants.

Definition of Virama – (। ॥ ,) danda, double danda, comma.

Visarga changes to ओ by रुत्व + उत्व + गुणसन्धिः

8.2.66 ससजुषोः रुँ ।
Final स् changes to र्

6.1.114 हशि च ।
र् preceded by अ and followed by हश् letter, changes to उ

6.1.87 आद्गुणः ।
When अवर्ण is followed by अच् any vowel, then both letters are replaced by the corresponding गुण letter.

Summary - Visarga [preceded by अ and followed by soft consonant or semivowel or aspirate] changes to ओ

e.g. verse 2.50 बुद्धियुक्तः जहातीह → 8.2.66 → बुद्धियुक्तर् जहातीह → 6.1.114 → बुद्धियुक्तउ जहातीह → 6.1.87 → बुद्धियुक्तो जहातीह

Definition of हश् – soft consonants, semivowels, aspirate
हश् – ग् घ् ङ् ज् झ् ञ् ड् ढ् ण् द् ध् न् ब् भ् म् , य् र् ल् व् , ह्
Definition of अच् – any vowel
अच् – अ आ इ ई उ ऊ , ऋ ॠ ऌ , ए ऐ ओ औ

Visarga changes to र्

6.1.114 हशि च ।

र् preceded by अ and followed by हश् letter, changes to उ

8.2.66 ससजुषोः रुँ ।

Final स् changes to र्

8.3.15 खर् अवसानयोः विसर्जनीयः ।

Appearance of Visarga.

- When a Final repha र् is followed by खर् hard consonant or a sibilant, Visarga appears in place of repha.
- Conversely, if final repha is not followed by खर् then instead of visarga the repha remains, only when repha is not preceded by अ (otherwise 6.1.114 shall apply)

In summary, Visarga [preceded by इच् and followed by हश्] changes to र्

Definition of इच् – any vowel except अ आ
Definition of हश् – soft consonant or semivowel or aspirate

e.g. 1.21, 1.24 सेनयोरुभयोः मध्ये → सेनयोरुभयोर् मध्ये → सेनयोरुभयोर्मध्ये
e.g. verse 1.32 भोगैः जीवितेन → भोगैर् जीवितेन → भोगैर्जीवितेन
e.g. verse 4.7 ग्लानिः भवति → ग्लानिर् भवति → ग्लानिर्भवति
e.g. verse 4.24 ब्रह्महविः ब्रह्माग्नौ → ब्रह्महविर् ब्रह्माग्नौ → ब्रह्महविर्ब्रह्माग्नौ

Visarga changes to श् when facing श् or चवर्ग

8.3.34 विसर्जनीयस्य सः ।

Visarga when followed by hard consonant, changes to स्

8.4.40 स्तोः श्चुना श्चुः ।

When स् faces श् the स् changes to श् , And

When स् faces a letter of चवर्ग, the स् changes to श् , And

When a letter of तवर्ग faces a letter of चवर्ग, the तवर्ग letter changes to corresponding letter of चवर्ग

e.g. verse 1.1 पाण्डवाः चैव → 8.3.34 → पाण्डवास् चैव → 8.4.40 → पाण्डवाश् चैव → पाण्डवाश्चैव

e.g. verse 1.9 बहवः शूरा → 8.3.34 → बहवस् शूरा → 8.4.40 → बहवश् शूरा → बहवश्शूरा

Visarga changes to स्

8.3.34 विसर्जनीयस्य सः ।

पदान्त Visarga when followed by खर् letter changes to स्

Definition of खर् – 1st 2nd letter of row consonants (hard consonants) and sibilant श् ष् स्

खर् – क् ख् च् छ् ट् ठ् त् थ् प् फ् श् ष् स्

Due to 8.4.40 खर् letters च् छ् श् give other results.

Due to 8.3.37 खर् letters क् ख् प् फ् give other results.

Ultimately, this rule can be summarized as - Visarga at end of a word when followed by त् थ् स् changes to स्

e.g. verse 2.55 स्थितप्रज्ञः तदोच्यते → 8.3.34 → स्थितप्रज्ञस् तदोच्यते → स्थितप्रज्ञस्तदोच्यते

Visarga gets dropped by रुत्व + यत्व + लोप

8.2.66 ससजुषोः रुँ ।

Final स् changes to रु

8.3.17 भोभगोअघोअपूर्वस्य योऽशि ।

रु preceded by अवर्ण changes to य् when followed by letter of अश् pratyahara.

> Note – By 6.1.114, when preceded by अकार, another sandhi takes effect, so this leaves us with आकार ।

8.3.22 हलि सर्वेषाम् ।

य् (that is made from रु) when followed by a consonant gets dropped

Summary
- *Visarga [preceded by अ and followed by vowel] gets dropped.*

e.g. verse 12.16 दक्षः उदासीनः→ 8.2.66 → दक्षरु उदासीनः → 8.3.17 →
दक्षय् उदासीनः → 8.3.22 → दक्ष उदासीनः

- *Visarga [preceded by आ and followed by vowel, soft consonant or semivowel or aspirate] gets dropped.*

e.g. verse 1.9 शूराः मदर्थे → 8.2.66 → शूरारु मदर्थे → 8.3.17 → शूराय् मदर्थे
→ 8.3.22 → शूरा मदर्थे

Definition of अश् – vowel, soft consonant, semivowel, aspirate
अश् – अ आ इ ई उ ऊ ऋ ॠ ऌ ए ऐ ओ औ , ग् घ् ङ् ज् झ् ञ् ड् ढ् ण् द् ध्
न् ब् भ् म् , य् र् ल् व् , ह्

Visarga may change to Ardhavisarga

8.3.37 कुप्वोः ○⤬क ⤬पौ च ।

Optionally
- Visarga to Ardhavisarga when followed by क् / ख् । This is called Jihvamuliya and hence enunciated as ह़
- Visarga to Ardhavisarga when followed by प् / फ् । This is called Upadhmaniya and hence enunciated as फ़

e.g. verse 1.1 मामकाः पाण्डवाश्चैव → 8.3.37 → मामका⤬ पाण्डवाश्चैव

e.g. verse 2.50 योगः कर्मसु → 8.3.37 → योग⤬ कर्मसु

Due to the Optional clause, *very few pandits chant it as an Ardhavisarga. So either recitation is valid.*

Visarga does not change to Ardhavisarga

8.3.35 शर्परे विसर्जनीयः ।

If a Visarga is followed by a खर् letter that is further followed by a शर् letter, then Visarga remains.

Definition of खर् - 1st 2nd letters of the class consonants क् ख् च् छ् ट् ठ् त् थ् प् फ् which are hard consonants, and श् ष् स् sibilants.

Definition of शर् - श् ष् स् sibilants.

Due to this rule, if visarga is followed by क्ष (क् ष्) then the ardhavisarga by 8.3.37 does not happen.

e.g. Verse 2.32 सुखिनः क्षत्रियाः , Verse 10.34 धृतिः क्षमा , Verse 12.13 समदुःखसुखः क्षमी , Verse 16.3 तेजः क्षमा

Panini's Ashtadhyayi Rules for Anusvara

Anusvara ◌ं is the result of a म् or न् । It is purely a nasal sound.

म् changes to Anusvara

8.3.23 मोऽनुस्वारः ।

- म् at end of a word (पदान्त) is replaced by Anusvara when a consonant follows.

- Conversely, if the following letter is a vowel, then the मकार remains unchanged.

This also means that if the following is a **pause**, then the मकार remains unchanged.

म् or न् changes to Anusvara

8.3.24 नश्चापदान्तस्य झलि ।

- म् or न् within a word (अपदान्त) will be replaced by Anusvara when a झल् letter follows.

Definition of झल् – all consonants except semivowels, nasals and the aspirate, i.e. 1st 2nd 3rd 4th letters of the class consonants and the sibilants.

e.g. verse 1.1   सञ्जय (संजय)

e.g. verse 1.15 महाशङ्ख्ं (महाशंखं)

Anusvara changes to Nasal

8.4.58 अनुस्वारस्य ययि परसवर्णः ।

For अपदान्त (within a word)

- Anusvara followed by a यय् letter will be replaced by a nasal of the row class of the following consonant.

- Anusvara followed by a semivowel will be replaced by its nasalized equivalent.

- In case repha र् is following, then Anusvara remains since there is no nasal equivalent for repha.

- In case sibilant श् ष् स् ह् is following, then Anusvara remains.

Definition of यय् = any row class consonant or semivowel.

Replacement for Anusvara = ङ् ञ् ण् न् म् यँ ़ लँ ़ वँ ़ ।

Anusvara may change to Nasal

8.4.59 वा पदान्तस्य ।

Optional For पदान्त (final letter of a word)
- The change to Nasal is Optional in case Anusvara is the final letter of a word, i.e. is in between two words.

Due to this rule, we find that Anusvara **within a word** is always changed to Nasal.

However when in between two words, i.e. the last letter of a word facing another word, some pandits chant it as a Nasal and others chant it as Anusvara. So either recitation is valid.

Visarga Anusvara Avagraha

Visarga Chanting Guidelines

The proper enunciation of Visarga is what makes the Gita chanting so powerful and revered. Be careful so that the following can be adhered to:

a) Visarga to हकार along with sound of previous vowel

b) Visarga to ओकार

c) Visarga to रेफ

d) Visarga to सकार

e) Visarga to शकार

f) Visarga to ह़ Jihvamuliya or फ़ Upadhmaniya

g) Visarga remains when facing क्ष and is hence chanted as हकार along with sound of previous vowel

h) Visarga gets dropped and is hence silent
i) A dropped Visarga reappears and must be chanted

Anusvara Chanting Guidelines

This rule is not so much enforced, *since most of us cannot pronounce the nasals precisely*. For most of us the Anusvara ं sounds just like म् and that is just fine for chanting.

If needed for precision, it is a good idea to chant Anusvara

- as ङ् when facing क् / ख्
- as ञ् when facing च् / ज्
- as न् when facing त् / थ् / द्

provided it is not placed on a conjunct and the following letter is not a conjunct.

Avagraha Chanting Guidelines

An avagraha ऽ is a silent letter and is not to be chanted. It is not given in Panini's Ashtadhyayi.

Avagraha relates to

- अकार replaced by आकार due to sandhi, ऽ
- आकार replaced by आकार due to sandhi, ऽऽ
- A dropped अकार due to sandhi, ऽ
- It is not used to indicate conjunct where previous word ends in halant and next word begins with अ / आ

A later renowned grammarian introduced it to prevent loss of meaning, when various languages became prevalent and Sanskrit texts became prone to misinterpretation.

e.g. verse 11.4 दर्शयात्मानमव्ययम् ॥

Here Avagraha will not be used, since words दर्शय , आत्मानम् , अव्ययम् are clear to someone who knows Sanskrit.

e.g. Verse 9.32 येऽपि - Here Avagraha may be used to indicate a dropped अकार due to sandhi. यः अपि

e.g. Verse 11.20 दृष्ट्वाऽद्भुतं - Avagraha may use. दृष्ट्वा अद्भुतं

e.g. Verse 13.29 तथाऽऽत्मानम् - Avagraha may use. तथा आत्मानम्

Sample Transliterated Verses

Here we give a sample verse from each chapter to enable enough practice for the Reader.

1 Yoga of Meeting Oneself

oṃ śrī paramātmane namaḥ | atha prathamo'dhyāyaḥ

Verse as written, with sandhis and conjuncts together
dhṛtarāṣṭra uvāca

dharmakṣetre kurukṣetre samavetā yuyutsavaḥ |

māmakāḥ pāṇḍavāścaiva kimakurvata sañjaya || 1

Verse as chanted, pausing at each pada quarter verse
dhṛtarāṣṭra uvāca

dharmakṣetre kurukṣetre , samavetā yuyut savaḥ |

māmakā× pāṇḍavāś caiva , kim akurvata sañjaya || 1.1

2 Yoga of Meeting The Lord

oṃ śrī paramātmane namaḥ | atha dvitīyo'dhyāyaḥ

Verse as written, with sandhis and conjuncts together
sañjaya uvāca
taṃ tathā kṛpayā'viṣṭamaśrupūrṇākulekṣaṇam |
viṣīdantamidaṃ vākyamuvāca madhusūdanaḥ ||

Verse as chanted, pausing at each pada quarter verse
sañjaya uvāca
taṃ tathā kṛpayāviṣṭam , aśrupūrṇākulekṣaṇam |
viṣīdantam idaṃ vākyam , uvāca madhusūdanaḥ || 2.1

3 Yoga of Right Choices in Life

oṃ śrī paramātmane namaḥ | atha tṛtīyo'dhyāyaḥ

Verse as written, with sandhis and conjuncts together
arjuna uvāca

jyāyasī cetkarmaṇaste matā buddhirjanārdana |

tatkiṃ karmaṇi ghore māṃ niyojayasi keśava || 1

Verse as chanted, pausing at each pada quarter verse
arjuna uvāca

jyāyasī cet karmaṇas te , matā buddhir janārdana |

tatkiṃ karmaṇi ghore mām , niyojayasi keśava || 3.1

4 Yoga of Intention

oṃ śrī paramātmane namaḥ | atha caturtho'dhyāyaḥ

Verse as written, with sandhis and conjuncts together
śrī bhagavānuvāca
imaṃ vivasvate yogaṃ proktavānahamavyayam |
vivasvānmanave prāha manurikṣvākave'bravīt ‖ 1

Verse as chanted, pausing at each pada quarter verse
śrī bhagavān uvāca
imaṃ vivasvate yogam , proktavān aham avyayam |
vivasvān manave prāha , manur ikṣvākavebravīt ‖ 4.1

5 Yoga of Calmness

oṃ śrī paramātmane namaḥ | atha pañcamo'dhyāyaḥ

Verse as written, with sandhis and conjuncts together
arjuna uvāca

sannyāsaṃ karmaṇāṃ kṛṣṇa punaryogaṃ ca śaṃsasi |

yacchreya etayorekaṃ tanme brūhi suniścitam ‖ 1

Verse as chanted, pausing at each pada quarter verse
arjuna uvāca

sannyāsaṃ karmaṇāṃ kṛṣṇa , punar yogaṃ ca śaṃsasi |

yacchreya etayorekam , tanme brūhi suniścitam ‖ 5.1

6 Yoga of Self Control

oṃ śrī paramātmane namaḥ | atha ṣaṣṭho'dhyāyaḥ

Verse as written, with sandhis and conjuncts together
śrī bhagavānuvāca
anāśritaḥ karmaphalaṃ kāryaṃ karma karoti yaḥ |
sa sannyāsī ca yogī ca na niragnirna cākriyaḥ || 1

Verse as chanted, pausing at each pada quarter verse
śrī bhagavān uvāca
anāśritaḥ karmaphalam , kāryaṃ karma karoti yaḥ |
sa sannyāsī ca yogī ca , na niragnir na cākriyaḥ || 6.1

7 Yoga of Divine Qualities

oṃ śrī paramātmane namaḥ | atha saptamo'dhyāyaḥ

Verse as written, with sandhis and conjuncts together
śrī bhagavānuvāca

mayyāsaktamanāḥ pārtha yogaṃ yuñjanmadāśrayaḥ |

asaṃśayaṃ samagraṃ māṃ yathā jñāsyasi tacchṛṇu ‖ 1

Verse as chanted, pausing at each pada quarter verse
śrī bhagavān uvāca

mayyāsaktamanāx pārtha , yogaṃ yuñjan madāśrayaḥ |

asaṃśayaṃ samagraṃ mām , yathā jñāsyasi tac chṛṇu ‖ 7.1

oṃ śrī paramātmane namaḥ | atha aṣṭamo'dhyāyaḥ

Verse as written, with sandhis and conjuncts together
arjuna uvāca

kiṃ tadbrahma kimadhyātmaṃ kiṃ karma puruṣottama |

adhibhūtaṃ ca kiṃ proktamadhidaivaṃ kimucyate ‖ 1

Verse as chanted, pausing at each pada quarter verse
arjuna uvāca

kiṃ tad brahma kim adhyātmam , kiṅ karma puruṣottama |

adhibhūtañ ca kiṃ proktam , adhidaivaṃ kim ucyate ‖ 8.1

9 Yoga of Royal Secrets

oṃ śrī paramātmane namaḥ | atha navamo'dhyāyaḥ

Verse as written, with sandhis and conjuncts together
śrī bhagavānuvāca
idaṃ tu te guhyatamaṃ pravakṣyāmyanasūyave |
jñānaṃ vijñānasahitaṃ yajjñātvā mokṣyase'śubhāt ‖ 1

Verse as chanted, pausing at each pada quarter verse
śrī bhagavān uvāca
idaṃ tu te guhyatamam , pravakṣyāmyanasūyave |
jñānaṃ vijñānasahitam , yaj jñātvā mokṣyaseśubhāt ‖ 9.1

10 Yoga of Divine Manifestations

oṃ śrī paramātmane namaḥ | atha daśamo'dhyāyaḥ

Verse as written, with sandhis and conjuncts together
śrī bhagavānuvāca

bhūya eva mahābāho śṛṇu me paramaṃ vacaḥ |

yatte'haṃ prīyamāṇāya vakṣyāmi hitakāmyayā || 1

Verse as chanted, pausing at each pada quarter verse
śrī bhagavān uvāca

bhūya eva mahābāho , śṛṇu me paramaṃ vacaḥ |

yatteham prīyamāṇāya , vakṣyāmi hitakāmyayā || 10.1

11 Yoga of The Cosmic Person

oṃ śrī paramātmane namaḥ | atha ekādaśo'dhyāyaḥ

Verse as written, with sandhis and conjuncts together
arjuna uvāca

madanugrahāya paramaṃ guhyamadhyātmasañjñitam |

yattvayoktaṃ vacastena moho'yaṃ vigato mama ‖ 1

Verse as chanted, pausing at each pada quarter verse
arjuna uvāca

madanugrahāya paramam , guhyam adhyātmasañjñitam |

yat tvayoktaṃ vacastena , mohoyaṃ vigato mama ‖ 11.1

oṃ śrī paramātmane namaḥ | atha dvādaśo'dhyāyaḥ

67

Verse as written, with sandhis and conjuncts together
arjuna uvāca

evaṃ satatayuktā ye bhaktāstvāṃ paryupāsate |

ye cāpyakṣaramavyaktaṃ teṣāṃ ke yogavittamāḥ || 1

Verse as chanted, pausing at each pada quarter verse
arjuna uvāca

evaṃ satatayuktā ye , bhaktās tvāṃ paryupāsate |

ye cāpyakṣaram avyaktam , teṣāṃ ke yogavittamāḥ || 12.1

13 Yoga of Matter and Consciousness

oṃ śrī paramātmane namaḥ | atha trayodaśo'dhyāyaḥ

Verse as written, with sandhis and conjuncts together
arjuna uvāca

prakṛtiṃ puruṣaṃ caiva kṣetraṃ kṣetrajñameva ca |

etadveditumicchāmi jñānaṃ jñeyaṃ ca keśava ||

Verse as chanted, pausing at each pada quarter verse
arjuna uvāca

prakṛtiṃ puruṣaṃ caiva , kṣetraṃ kṣetrajñam eva ca |

etad veditum icchāmi , jñānaṃ jñeyaṃ ca keśava ||
Some editions of the Gita have this verse.
It changes the verse count from 700 to 701.

śrī bhagavānuvāca

idaṃ śarīraṃ kaunteya kṣetramityabhidhīyate |

etadyo vetti taṃ prāhuḥ kṣetrajña iti tadvidaḥ || 1
śrī bhagavān uvāca

idaṃ śarīraṃ kaunteya , kṣetram ityabhidhīyate |

etad yo vetti taṃ prāhuḥ , kṣetrajña iti tadvidaḥ || 13.1

14 Yoga of Three Creative Energies

oṃ śrī paramātmane namaḥ | atha caturdaśo'dhyāyaḥ

Verse as written, with sandhis and conjuncts together

śrī bhagavānu uvāca

paraṃ bhūyaḥ pravakṣyāmi jñānānāṃ jñānamuttamam |

yajjñātvā munayaḥ sarve parāṃ siddhimito gatāḥ ‖ 1

Verse as chanted, pausing at each pada quarter verse

śrī bhagavānu uvāca

paraṃ bhūyaḥ pravakṣyāmi , jñānānāṃ jñānam uttamam |

yaj jñātvā munayas sarve , parāṃ siddhim ito gatāḥ ‖ 14.1

15 Yoga of The Ideal Man

oṃ śrī paramātmane namaḥ l atha pañcadaśo'dhyāyaḥ

Verse as written, with sandhis and conjuncts together
śrī bhagavānuvāca
ūrdhvamūlamadhaḥśākhamaśvatthaṃ prāhuravyayam l
chandāṃsi yasya parṇāni yastaṃ veda sa vedavit ll 1

Verse as chanted, pausing at each pada quarter verse
śrī bhagavān uvāca
ūrdhvamūlam adhaḥśākham , aśvatthaṃ prāhur avyayam l
chandāṃsi yasya parṇāni , yastaṃ veda sa vedavit ll 15.1

adhaścordhvaṃ prasṛtāstasya śākhā
guṇapravṛddhā viṣayapravālāḥ l
adhaśca mūlānyanusantatāni
karmānubandhīni manuṣyaloke ll 2
adhaś cordhvaṃ prasṛtās tasya śākhāḥ ,
guṇapravṛddhā viṣayapravālāḥ l
adhaśca mūlānyanusantatāni ,
karmānubandhīni manuṣyaloke ll 15.2 Trishtup

16 Yoga of Good and Bad Habits

oṃ śrī paramātmane namaḥ ׀ atha ṣoḍaśo'dhyāyaḥ

Verse as written, with sandhis and conjuncts together
śrī bhagavānuvāca
abhayaṃ sattvasaṃśuddhirjñānayogavyavasthitiḥ ׀
dānaṃ damaśca yajñaśca svādhyāyastapa ārjavam ׀׀ 1

Verse as chanted, pausing at each pada quarter verse
śrī bhagavān uvāca
abhayaṃ sattvasaṃśuddhiḥ , jñānayogavyavasthitiḥ ׀
dānaṃ damaśca yajñaśca , svādhyāyas tapa ārjavam ׀׀ 16.1

17 Yoga of Sattva Rajas Tamas

oṃ śrī paramātmane namaḥ ǀ atha saptadaśo'dhyāyaḥ

Verse as written, with sandhis and conjuncts together
arjuna uvāca
ye śāstravidhimutsṛjya yajante śraddhayā'nvitāḥ ǀ
teṣāṃ niṣṭhā tu kā kṛṣṇa sattvamāho rajastamaḥ ǀǀ 1

Verse as chanted, pausing at each pada quarter verse
arjuna uvāca
ye śāstravidhim utsṛjya , yajante śraddhayānvitāḥ ǀ
teṣāṃ niṣṭhā tu kā kṛṣṇa , sattvam āho rajas tamaḥ ǀǀ 17.1

18 Yoga of Liberation

oṃ śrī paramātmane namaḥ | atha aṣṭādaśo'dhyāyaḥ

Verse as written, with sandhis and conjuncts together
arjuna uvāca
sannyāsasya mahābāho tattvamicchāmi veditum |
tyāgasya ca hṛṣīkeśa pṛthakkeśiniṣūdana || 1

Verse as chanted, pausing at each pada quarter verse
arjuna uvāca
sannyāsasya mahābāho , tattvam icchāmi veditum |
tyāgasya ca hṛṣīkeśa , pṛthak keśiniṣūdana || 18.1

---

oṃ tat sat |
iti śrīmadbhagavadgītāsu upaniṣatsu brahmavidyāyāṃ
yogaśāstre śrīkṛṣṇārjunasaṃvāde mokṣa-sannyāsa-yogo
nāma aṣṭādaśo'dhyāyaḥ || 18th ||

---

gurur brahmā gurur viṣṇuḥ , gurur devo maheśvaraḥ |
gurus sākṣāt paraṃ brahma , tasmai śrīgurave namaḥ ||
śrī gurubhyo namaḥ hariḥ oṃ |
śrī kṛṣṇārpaṇamastu ||

Latin Transliteration Chart

International Alphabet of Sanskrit Transliteration (I.A.S.T.)

a	ā	i	ī	u	ū	r̥	r̥̄	l̥	
अ	आ	इ	ई	उ	ऊ	ऋ	ॠ	ऌ	
						ृ	ॄ	ॢ	
e	ai	o	au	ṃ	m̐	ḥ	Ardha Visarga	oṃ	
ए	ऐ	ओ	औ	◌ं	◌ँ	◌ः	◌ꣳ	ॐ	

Consonants are shown with a vowel 'a = अ' for uttering

ka	क	ca	च	ṭa	ट	ta	त	pa	प
kha	ख	cha	छ	ṭha	ठ	tha	थ	pha	फ
ga	ग	ja	ज	ḍa	ड	da	द	ba	ब
gha	घ	jha	झ	ḍha	ढ	dha	ध	bha	भ
ṅa	ङ	ña	ञ	ṇa	ण	na	न	ma	म

ya	ra	la	va		ḷa	'			
य	र	ल	व		ळ	s			
						Consonant only			
śa	ṣa	sa	ha		ka	क्अ = क			
श	ष	स	ह		k	क्			

Maheshwar Sutras

माहेश्वराणि सूत्राणि are sounds that are a rearrangement of the Devanagari Alphabet for grammatical use. Listed at the start of the Ashtadhyayi Sutrapatha.

1	अइउण्	All vowels = अच्
2	ऋऌक्	Simple vowels = अक्
3	एओङ्	Diphthongs = एच्
4	ऐऔच्	Semivowels = यण्
5	हयवरट्	All consonants = हल्
6	लँण्	ल्+अँ, No nasal for र्
7	अमङणनम्	5th of row = Nasals = अम्
8	झभञ्	4th of row = झष्
9	घढधष्	are all soft consonants
10	जबगडदश्	3rd of row = जश् (soft)
11	खफछठथचटतव्	1st and 2nd of row = खय्
12	कपय्	are all hard consonants
13	शषसर्	Sibilants (hard) = शर्
14	हल्	Aspirate is soft

Consonants have been written with अकार solely for enunciation. But the लँण् = ल् अँ ण् contains लकार, anunasika Tag अँ, and a consonant Tag ण् ।

Maheshwar Sutras Elucidated

			The magic		
1	अ इ उ	ण्	All vowels = अच्	All vowels	Simple vowels
2	ऋ ऌ	क्	Simple vowels = अक्		
3	ए ओ	ङ्	Diphthongs = एच्		diphthongs
4	ऐ औ	च्	Semivowels = यण्		
5	ह य व र	ट्	All consonants = हल्	All consonants	Aspirate & Semi vowels
6	ल	ण्			
7	अ म ङ ण न	म्	5th of row = all Nasals = अम्		nasals
8	झ भ	ञ्	4th of row = झष्		Maha prana
9	घ ढ ध	ष्	= are soft consonants		
10	ज ब ग ड द	श्	3rd of row = जश् (soft consonants)		Alpa prana
11	ख फ छ ठ थ च ट त	व्	1st and 2nd of row = खय्		1st and 2nd of row
12	क प	य्	= are hard consonants		
13	श ष स	र्	Sibilants are hard consonants = शर्		
14	ह	ल्	Aspirate is soft consonant		

			Mouth Tongue Position	
1	अ इ उ	ण्	Guttural, palatal, labial	Simple vowels
2	ऋ ऌ	क्	Cerebral, dental	
3	ए ओ	ङ्	Gutturo-palatal, gutturo-labial	diphthongs
4	ऐ औ	च्	Gutturo-palatal, gutturo-labial	
5	ह य व र	ट्	Guttural, dento-labial, dento-labial, dento-labial	Aspirate & semivowels
6	ल	ण्	dento-labial अन्तःस्थः	
7	ञ म ङ ण न	म्	Palatal, labial, guttural, cerebral, dental	nasals
8	झ भ	ञ्	Palatal, labial	Maha prana
9	घ ढ ध	ष्	Guttural, cerebral, dental	
10	ज ब ग ड द	श्	Palatal, labial, guttural, cerebral, dental	Alpa prana
11	ख फ छ ठ थ च ट त	व्	Guttural, labial, palatal, cerebral, dental, palatal, cerebral, dental	Maha prana
12	क प	य्	Guttural, labial	Alpa prana
13	श ष स	र्	Sibilants – उष्माण: hot	Alpa prana
14	ह	ल्	Aspirate – breathe in	Maha prana

Pratyaharas

SN	Maheshwar Sutras	Pratyaharas	Count
1	अइउण्	अण्	1
2	ऋऌक्	अक् इक् उक्	3
3	एओङ्	एङ्	1
4	ऐऔच्	अच् इच् एच् ऐच्	4
5	हयवरट्	अट्	1
6	लँण्	अण् इण् यण् रँ	3
7	अमङणनम्	अम् यम् ङम् अम्	3
8	झभञ्	यञ्	1
9	घढधष्	झष् भष्	2
10	जबगडदश्	अश् हश् वश् झश् जश् बश्	6
11	खफछठथँचटतव्	छव् खँ	1
12	कपय्	यय् मय् झय् खय् चय् जय्	4
13	शषसर्	यर् झर् खर् चर् शर्	5
14	हल्	अल् हल् वल् रल् झल् शल्	6
		Basic Count of Pratyaharas =	41
	Extended Count 41 + 3 = 44 + 2 with later grammarians =		46

References

Mani Bhaiya sings the Gita https://artofliving.app/

Padmini Chandrashekhar sings the Gita
https://www.youtube.com/watch?v=kO8Bbg6wTHs

Lata Mangeshkar sings the Gita
https://www.youtube.com/watch?v=irqkpb-1Jmc

Swami Brahmananda sings the Gita
https://www.youtube.com/watch?v=HN5f2CGKmXk

Swami Paramarthananda sings the Gita
https://www.youtube.com/watch?v=dOigTv93CG8

Bangalore Ashram Vaidic Pujas
https://www.youtube.com/watch?v=KOlYCkN88-0

Ashwini Kumar Aggarwal
– Bhagavad Gita Reader: All verses in 4 Quarters – 1st – 2017
– Sanskrit Sandhi Handbook – 1st – 2019
Ashwini Kumar Aggarwal and Sadhvi Hemswaroopa
- Bhagavad Gita as Recited vs as Written – 1st – 2022
Devotees of Sri Sri Ravi Shankar Ashram, Punjab.

Bhagavad Gita Chanting Books
https://www.amazon.com/dp/1521063370/
https://books.apple.com/us/book/bhagavad-gita-reader/id1405805937
https://play.google.com/store/books/details?id=94I4DwAAQBAJ
https://play.google.com/store/books/details?id=kt1hEAAAQBAJ
https://www.zorbabooks.com/store/religion/bhagavad-gita-recitation/

Epilogue

The Bhagavad Gita is a tour de force. It is the complete manual for emotional, physical and financial success on the human plane.

It can heal any trauma, it can revive any relationship, it can make any target achievable. It is the family's best companion, equally relevant for young children, excited teenagers, hard pressed working adults, or the retired seniors.

सर्वे भवन्तु सुखिनः । सर्वे सन्तु निरामयाः ।

सर्वे भद्राणि पश्यन्तु । मा कश्चिद् दुःख भाग् भवेत् ॥

ॐ शान्तिः शान्तिः शान्तिः ॥

When faith has blossomed in life, Every step is led by the Divine.

Sri Sri Ravi Shankar

Om Namah Shivaya

जय गुरुदेव

www.ingramcontent.com/pod-product-compliance
Lightning Source LLC
LaVergne TN
LVHW021322200726
843509LV00002B/93